VANISHED HOUSES of North Devon

Rosemary Ann

First published in 1981
by Rosemary Anne Lauder
Designed, typeset and printed in Great Britain
by Penwell Ltd., Parkwood, Callington, Cornwall.

ISBN 0 9507920 04

Page

Introduction

There is something endlessly fascinating about a deserted dwelling. Crumbling stonework, gaping doorways, empty windows. Overgrown drives, unkempt grass, ever-encroaching wilderness. Only the crows in the trees to break the silence. Is it the romance of a ruin, or the aura of mystery that arouses nostalgia? Or is it the sense of loss, that where once all was noise and bustle, where people lived and loved, laughed and died, all is now solitude and desolation? It must be so, for the unlevelled grassy site of a former mansion can prove as powerfully evocative as the most romantic ruin.

Of such sites North Devon has its share.

Some will argue that the loss of a few tons of crumbling stonework are of no importance, but the country house is a very English institution, and quite apart from the nostalgic element, played a large part in the social history of our country.

North Devon has never been a wealthy area. The agricultural land is not good, the climate is wet and inhospitable, the villages often mean and untidy. Large country houses were few and far between and many of those that were built have now vanished from the scene.

In this book I have attempted to record six of those vanished houses, once landmarks in the North Devon countryside. Memories grow short, younger generations are disinterested, and much of the documentation is lost for ever, thrown out as so many old photographs or papers with no present day significance. I have tried to collect together such material as still survives and, before memories fade completely, talk to those who knew and worked in them.

Of the six Stevenstone, Eggesford and Winscott were Victorian mansions, huge, rambling and totally impracticable today. They were a statement of their owners' importance and wealth, and all were obsolescent within one hundred years of their building.

Annery House was smaller and of an earlier period and had it survived the neglect of the post-war era would have continued its life as a hotel or been sub-divided.

For Yeo Vale there was no chance of a reprieve. It was allowed to become a dangerous ruin because its owner deserted it, and could not therefore be sold.

Only Dunsland House was accidentally lost, destroyed by fire just as it was about to take up its position as one of the premier properties owned by the National Trust in the Westcountry.

Ruins of two of the largest survive, but for the others flattened grassy areas surrounded by derelict parkland or decaying outbuildings are the only clue to the former existence of a once noble country seat.

The country house reached its zenith in the nineteenth century. The Victorian era was one of great change. Communications had improved considerably. The old rutted cart tracks that had served for so long had been replaced by modern turn-pikes, and the coming of the railway brought distant counties such as Devon, within reach of the Capital. Travel suddenly became a pleasure instead of penance to be avoided at all costs and undertaken only when absolutely necessary.

Wealth at the beginning of the nineteenth century was still mainly in the hands of the landed gentry, who had ruled England under a patriarchal system going back for centuries. But a new class was springing up who owed their wealth to the new factories and industries of the North and Midlands. Their passport to polite society was either a nobly-born wife or, at the very least, a country seat. So began the spate of building that reached its peak in the middle of the century.

Although the happenings in the industrial north had little immediate effect on North Devon, the fashion for buildings rubbed off. Before the great agricultural depression that affected landowners all over the country in the 1880's, the landed gentry were accumulating vast wealth from their tenants. Many of those who could now afford to do so, decided to replace their modest family seats, or at least enlarge and embellish them. Both Stevenstone and Eggesford were examples of this Victorian desire to keep up with the Joneses; Eggesford a completely new house, Stevenstone an old one enlarged and rebuilt beyond recognition.

Morals, too, had undergone a change. Whereas before life below stairs was previously a hit and miss affair of not much concern to the owner, Victorian standards dictated that the behaviour and code of conduct of the servants was as much the responsibility of the employer as those of his own family. Male and female servants were strictly segregated, preferably in separate wings with separate staircases. Even the guests' accommodation ideally would be in bachelor and female corridors. Modern inventions meant changes in the old-fashioned kitchens. New sculleries, cold rooms, laundries and boiler rooms were needed. The love of everything well ordered required separate rooms for the boots, for the silver, for the cutlery, for the china, for the lamps, for the butler, for the housekeeper. The number of servants needed to keep such an establishment going was much greater than before and this in turn generated a need for yet more rooms.

It was, too, a great age for visiting. "The weekend" was born in the days of Victoria and country house parties were frequent and enormous, right up until the first world war, with guests often bringing a retinue of servants. Just as the industrial revolution left Devon largely unaffected, so too did the agricultural depression. Upcountry, large estates floundered and many of the old families were reduced to penury. The succession of bad harvests, cheap imports and depressed agricultural markets must have taken their toll, but the principal estates survived. Nor did the two world wars directly affect the occupants of the six houses.

Indirectly they were all lost because of the tremendous change in social climate caused by those years of devastation. No-one wanted the large out-dated houses, needing an army of servants and a mountain of cash. The servants were no longer available and rising taxation, death duties and falling markets had drastically reduced the cash resources.

Directly the loss of four, and very nearly five, out of the six houses can be attributed to those magnificent timbered acres, of which their owners were so proud, planted by a generation of caring forbears not only to beautify their estates but to provide a steady source of income for their heirs. Chain saws, that invention of the devil, within months could reduce to sticks of timber the growth of centuries. Once an estate had been divided and the valuable farmland and timber sold off, it became a virtual impossibility to maintain the house. The centre and kingpin of so many activities and so many lives had lost its purpose as well as the source of wealth needed to maintain it. There are still clues, still reminders. The former lodge houses along the roadside, the entrance gates that open on to nothing, the drive that now pointlessly leads across a few fields, and the few surviving trees that graced the former parkland. And a few old prints hung on cottage walls, a few old postcards tucked away in drawers . . . .

STEVENSTONE

Sufficient remains of Stevenstone to give some idea of its former magnificence. Of all the large houses in North Devon, this must have been by far the largest, and the most unusual. Even after half the original house had been demolished it remained a large property with 27 bedrooms and 4 reception rooms. In design, the house resembled a French chateau, with steeply pitched roof in which were set the windows of the first floor, and turreted towers at each corner.

The ruins are very much the memorial to one man and to his unshakeable Victorian faith in the continuance of their way of life and the supremacy of the wealthy landowner classes. But Stevenstone lasted less than one hundred years and within fifty had become a white elephant, a nostalgic symbol of a vanished era.

The Hon. Mark Rolle was that man. Born Mark George Kerr Trefusis, the second son of Baron Clinton and Lady Elizabeth Georgina Kerr, he inherited the estate from Lord John Rolle who died in 1842, changing his name to Rolle by Royal Licence in 1852 when he was 17. At the age of 33, in 1868, he began building the new Stevenstone, an ambitious project for so young a man, and one which was to take over four years to complete. The total cost was reputed to have been £28,000.

Very few records remain of the great house, but one or two prints survive that show Stevenstone in its heyday. The architect was believed to have been C.M. Barrie, son of the Barrie responsible for the Houses of Parliament.

A contemporary report describes the house:

> "Stevenstone House is most pleasant to look upon. It is of fresh coloured stone, with Tisbury dressings, all the windows being of square design, the upper ones have pediments. The style of architecture might be called 'French Italian.' In front of the house, which faces south, and extending the whole width, is a straight, open stone balustrade, which is continued at the west end in a semi-circular sweep, enclosing the finely kept tennis ground. At both the east and west ends stands a tower. Another tower stands near the east end, terminating with pinnacles. A large flag-staff rises from the centre. These towers, together with the turrets over the stables adjoining, help to give the building an imposing appearance."

The balustrade that separated grounds from parkland, remains almost intact; the tennis ground is still discernible although no longer 'finely kept' and the stables have been converted into

Stevenstone in 1872

dwellings. But the house itself, in all its 'French Italian' glory is nothing but a dangerous, overgrown ruin.

The new Stevenstone must have been a most up-to-date house when completed. A gas plant was installed in 1873 with telescopic gas holders, retorts and hoppers and gas engines drove the workshop machinery. The house had a service lift, central heating, telephone (Torrington 24), and an elaborate system of fire hoses. A whole colony of outhouses, workshops, sawmills and stabling grew up to the rear. The stables were particularly handsome, horses and hunting being Mark Rolle's main interest. Several new drives were constructed connecting the new house with the principal roads, each with its own lodge. All six lodges survive, although only two of the drives are in use.

Entertainment at Stevenstone was on a lavish scale. Shooting parties, usually four a year, were very popular with the local population as many of them were employed to help with the sudden influx of guests. It was the era of country-house weekends, and Mark Rolle was a hospitable host. During the cold winters of that age, so much colder than those of today, when the lake predictably froze, skating parties were held. On one occasion Mark Rolle hired a Hungarian band which happened to be in the area to play for his guests as they skated.

But the highlight of the year was the Stevenstone annual flower show, held on the last Thursday in July. A colony of marquees and tents sprang up in the grounds. There were dancing platforms, a tea tent and numerous side shows. Preparations went on for weeks beforehand and the excitement and competition must have been intense amongst the local population. Many of them still remember the flower show and the fun that everyone had there. In that pre-war age when everything conformed, including the weather, no doubt the sun always shone from a clear, blue sky on the day of the Stevenstone show.

Mark Rolle's Stevenstone replaced a much older house on the same site, part of which must have been incorporated in the new building. An old print shows a plain, rectangular manor house, without the terrace but in very much the same position. Of this earlier house there are virtually no records, but a manor house existed in 1309 when Margery, wife of Richard, son of Sir Richard de Stapledon had a licence for divine service in the chapel at Stevenstone. Ancient records give the first known holder of the

Stevenstone — an old print.

manor as one Michael de St. Stephens. Other names include a Richard St. Michael, Basset, De la Ley, Grant and Moyle. During the reign of Henry VIII the estate was bought by George Rolle. He died in 1552 and the estate passed to his son John, died in 1570 and to his son Sir Henry, died 1625. The next heir, another Sir Henry, united the Stevenstone and Bicton estates by marrying the co-heiress, Anne Dennys. Their son, Dennys or Denys succeeded in 1617, and on his death in 1638 was buried at Bicton. His only son died young in 1642. A descendant of the original John Rolle, Henry Rolle of Beam, near Torrington, was the next owner, but died in 1647 without issue. Sir John Rolle, another branch of the family, succeeded and married Florence Rolle, daughter of Denys Rolle. When he died in 1706 he owned 45 manors in Devon and Cornwall. His two sons both predeceased him and his estates passed to his grandson John, who died in 1730. Of his four sons, three died without issue, but the eldest Henry, was created a Baron in 1748. He died unmarried and was succeeded in turn by his brothers John and Denys, who already owned large estates from his mother. Denys was an ambitious man who attempted to colonise Florida in America, but the enterprise was not a success. Anne Chichester of Hall, Bishops Tawton, was his wife and it was their son, John, Lord Rolle, Baron of Stevenstone, who died in 1842, at the age of 92. He left his Bicton estates to his wife, the Hon. Louisa Trefusis, daughter of Lord Clinton, and Stevenstone passed to his nephew the Hon. Mark Rolle.

Mark Rolle died in 1907, six years after Queen Victoria's long reign had ended. His widow, Lady Gertrude, died in 1924, aged 86, and, in company with many of their forbears, both are buried in the family vaults at the parish church of St. Giles-in-the-Wood. The greater part of this village was built by Mark Rolle to house the army of estate workers.

Stevenstone was bought by Captain and Mrs. Clemson in 1912. She was a member of the McKinnon family and supposedly an heiress. Immediately they set about reducing their new home to more manageable proportions. But Capt. Clemson was killed at Gallipoli in December, 1915 and never returned to his wife and baby daughter.

The entire east front was demolished, including the main tower and one of the corner towers, thus destroying the symmetry of the southern front, itself reduced to half its former length. The windows

Stevenstone in 1930

and door mouldings were retained and used in the new facade. The main entrance doorway is still there with its wide flight of steps but, alas, the caller is greeted, not by a well-kept hallway with polished floors and bowls of flowers, but by a sheer drop straight down into the cellars, with brambles and weeds covering the fallen debris.

The demolition necessitated some changes in ground levels. The site of the former front was filled in and a wide grassed terrace created. A new curving ramp was constructed leading down to the stables so that carriages could pull up by the entrance steps. Mrs. Clemson remarried a Col. B.C. James, and for a while life continued at Stevenstone very much as before. The kennels of the Stevenstone hunt were still located in the grounds and many local people remember the grand opening meet held each year under the terrace of the big house, one of the major events of the social and sporting calendar.

The only clear description of the interior of the house comes, once again, from sale particulars. On 26th September, 1930 the

"Sporting, residential and agricultural estate of Stevenstone, extending to about 665 acres and including the important mansion, suitable for an Hotel, Country Club, Institution or School" was offered for auction. The particulars describe a billiards room, 50 feet by 20 feet, a panelled entrance hall, 35 feet by 20 feet with adjoining panelled staircase hall, a dining room, 33 feet by 18 feet, a drawing room of similar size and a more modest smoking room. Upstairs were 14 bed or dressing rooms with four bathrooms, three with heated towel rails and three separate W.C.'s. Five servant's bedrooms and a bathroom were located in a separate wing and a further bachelor wing on the ground floor contained a further four bedrooms and two bathrooms. The menservants had four bedrooms and a bathroom in the lower ground floor. A 16 h.p. Hornsby engine provided electric light. The stable block, built round an open courtyard, contained a 6-stall stable, three blocks of loose boxes for eight, seven and four horses, harness and grooms' rooms and range of four grooms' bedrooms. In addition there was garaging for 10 cars.

Billiard Room and Lounge

Dining Room

The estate was again up for auction in May, 1931 and was described as "lately the residence of the late Col. B.C. James." The total amount of land offered was considerably less than the preceding year and it is not clear whether the house failed to find a buyer in 1930, or was purchased and again offered for sale at £3,000 a year later, when it remained unsold. A press cutting from the Western Times of 29th May read:

Under the Hammer but Not Sold

Stevenstone House, a well-known North Devon mansion at St. Giles-in-the-Wood, near Torrington, was offered at auction at the Globe Hotel, Torrington, on Saturday, by Messrs. John Smale and Co., of Barnstaple, in conjunction with Messrs. W. J. Slee and Son, of Torrington. The mansion, lately the residence of the late Col. B. C. James, Master of the Stevenstone Foxhounds, was offered with grounds extending to about 17 acres.

The mansion is a modern building, some sixty years old, incorporating part of the house built in the first half of the 16th century by Geo. Rolle. It was built by the Hon. Mark Rolle, who resided there for many years, and was completed in 1873 at a cost of £28,000. In later years considerable sums had been spent on improvements. The house, overlooking a magnificently timbered park, contains 4 reception-rooms, 27 bed and dressing-rooms and eight bathrooms, and in the grounds a rose garden and much-prized pinetum.

The lot was offered at the upset price of £3,000, but did not find a buyer.

Of the remainder of the estate, extending to nearly 300 acres, a number of the lots had been sold by the auctioneers privately. The deer park, with a chain of fish ponds, the whole extending to 108 acres, was knocked down to Mr. W. J. Slee at £1,000. and Mr. Gilbert Hookway bought a building at St. Giles now used by the Skittling Club for £12, stating he had bought it for the parish. A few other lots were withdrawn.

The Stevenstone Kennels were announced by the auctioneers to have been withdrawn from the sale, the Stevenstone Hunt having been promised the first refusal and certain cottages known as the almshouses were also withdrawn.

The solicitors concerned were Messrs. Bazeley, Barnes and Bazeley, Bideford.

Western Times **29th May, 1931**

Perhaps the house failed to attract a buyer because so much of the "magnificently timbered park" had been sold for an undisclosed sum to Bartlett's of Bideford, a timber company. The death knell had been rung for Stevenstone.

Less than four months later the entire structure was offered for sale, split up into over 600 lots.

At some time during that summer Stevenstone had been bought by Mr. John Millman of Winscott Barton, at St. Giles. He decided to break up the old house and a catalogue of fixtures and fittings "to be sold previous to the demolition of the mansion" was issued.

The Estate was divided and sold off, the parkland split up but no-one wanted the home of the Rolles. Without its supporting land and

The Hunt outside the main entrance with the servant's wing on the right

farms the great house was like a beached whale, gasping for breath and waiting for its inevitable end. The catalogue lists some interesting lots. As well as numerous marble fireplaces and over 100 pine-panelled doors, offered for sale were 3,300 square feet of oak panelling and dado and 11,000 square feet of oak and pine flooring. Another lot was the dining room ceiling, described as decorated with an oval of raised fruit and flowers, also a frieze with cupids, birds, fruit and flowers. The staircase, described as "massive oak" had 24 treads and risers 4 feet 9 inches wide, with 51 feet and 6 inches of handrail, 14 newel posts and two half landings. Everything was to go — curtain rails, light fittings, baths, even the white glazed tiles on the walls.

Lot 609 was the remaining shell of the mansion "as it will stand after the sale of the fixtures and fittings with the whole of the excellent floor joists and roof timbers, including roofing slates and lead, the whole of the stone and brickwork including window and door frames."

Colonel James on Tetcott

But Stevenstone was repreived. Mr. Millman decided about a quarter way through the sale that he could not bear the prospect of the house being broken up. Unable to actually halt the sale, he bought back what he could, hoping to find a buyer for the house as it was. For many years the great building stood, shuttered and empty, whilst all around the once beautiful woodlands, were felled.

In an attempt to reduce the house to a more saleable size, Mr. Millman demolished the servant's wing that connected the mansion with the stable block, but still no buyer came forward.

For a brief period life came back to the house once more when the Warwickshire regiment and later, American troops, were billeted there during the Second World War. The house must have been habitable despite the sale and the ensuing years of neglect. At the end of the war old Mr. Millman wanted to settle his affairs. According to his son, Douglas, he decided to sell Stevenstone, having no use for it. Mr. Douglas Millman still remembers how shocked his father was when he discovered that the purchaser, Mr.

Melville, intended to knock the old house down and not convert it into flats as he believed.

What happened next is a familiar story. The house was never demolished completely, but anything that could be sold was stripped off and the fabric gradually "nibbled away" until only the ruinous shell was left. Much of the stone work and brick went to help in the conversion of Stevenstone's handsome stable block into mews-type houses. In addition several bungalows were built in the former kitchen gardens with the result that although the central core and heart of the estate has gone, Stevenstone still supports a large community and is still very much alive.

One of those new bungalows, built in 1962 less than 100 yards from the ruined house, is owned by Mr. Roy Parnell. Old Stevenstone had always fascinated him — his father-in-law had bought the Deer Park in 1931 — and around 1970 Mr. Parnell bought what was left of the house. He collected antiques, he said, and this one was right on his doorstep and he was especially fond of it.

The sunk garden and stable block

From his garden, Mr. Parnell has direct access to the cellars through a tunnel under the terrace. This was a well-hidden tradesmens' entrance, allowing servants to carry on their tasks unhindered and out of sight of their employers. By keeping close to the terrace wall they could pass to and fro from the stables and workshops, unseen from the house. The Victorians liked a well ordered house, but preferred it to be achieved as if by magic, the perfect servant being invisible.

Much of the below-stairs area is filled with rubble and overgrown, but the bones of the house are discernible. Parts of the walls seem to predate the rest of the structure, being of very small brick, and could possibly be the remnants of the earlier house. Another discovery was the pump handle by the "below-stairs" entrance probably sited above the well that supplied much of the needs of the household. Several of the very heavy metal counterweights used to operate the large sashwindows have been found amongst the rubble, and Mr. Parnell has a sizeable collection of glass seals bearing the Rolle crest, many of which he has dug up in his garden. Wine bought in quantity from a vineyard was often bottled and sealed for the noble purchaser in this way.

The construction of Stevenstone incorporated one unusual feature. Between the main external walls of the house and the made-up ground of the terraces a sizeable gap was left, forming a tunnel. Mr. Parnell remembers crawling along the tunnel throughout its entire length, following the lines of the original house, and much of it is still traceable, either from the basement or through the gratings at ground level. Presumably the intention of the architect was to keep damp away from the main fabric of the house, but Mr. Parnell likes to think it served a secondary purpose. The tunnel can be entered from the main servants' entrance under the east front. At one point on the west front a small staircase rises from the tunnel and in the thickness of the wall a small doorway has been cut with its own steps leading up to the garden. This, Mr. Parnell, thinks, would have been an ideal route for those who wished to come and go unseen!

The Library

Obviously much older than the house itself, the library is a separate and most unusual building. Built in the style of Queen Anne and probably regarded by Mark Rolle as a shabby, old-

Miss Margaret Clemson and her mother Mrs. James at the Stevenstone Hunt Ball 1935.

fashioned 'out-house' it is this small building that is historically listed and has recently been carefully restored, whilst the imposing modern mansion lies in ruins.

At one time owned by Mr. Millman's sister, it was sold at auction in July, 1978, to the Landmark Trust, who have since spent many thousands of pounds on repairs, thus ensuring the future of this charming building. The library looks out across the former tennis courts and indeed, at one time its main function seems to have been as a pavilion for both cricketers and tennis players, providing changing rooms and a setting for lavish teas. In those days the ground floor was not enclosed, the arches only being filled in when the library was converted into a dwelling. Its facade, with tall windows, matching colonnades and shallow roof, is small but perfectly in scale and gives something of the air of a dolls house alongside its large neighbour. Before its conversion, the upper floor was one large room lit by five sash windows, lined with oak panelling and shutters. The marble fireplace with oak overmantle and the fine moulded ceiling have been preserved. The room was lined with bookcases, 12 feet tall, of oak with inlay, all of which were sold off, but one found a home with Mr. Millman at Winscott Barton.

Behind the library was a small garden with a rose covered pergola of 22 arches leading to the orangery, another small building of great charm, but in a ruinous state when the Landmark Trust took over. This was probably the arbour referred to in the following description of the gardens in their prime:

> "Beautiful trees of the fir tribe grace the gardens. Attractive is the bed of bamboos and acanthus and near it is a large species of paulonia from seed gathered in the South of France some years ago by Lady Gertrude Rolle, and which flowered for the first time last spring. The avenue of fuchsias look distinctly rich and there is a very good collection of climbing roses on arches and standards of iron work leading to an open arbour covered with roses and clematis. Fan palms lend a tropical look to the surroundings. The lower flower garden is equally effective with its beds of salvias, fucshias, begonias, petunias, verbenas, heliotropes etc. while the rockery and fish ponds give a finish to this part of the grounds."

The woodland surrounding the library is sadly overgrown, but one or two remnants of the pinetum, much famed in its day, remain.

The grounds have suffered many changes since the red deer grazed in front of the mansion. The sale of much of the land to a timber company resulted in the almost total denudation of the estate. Hundreds of acres of fine mature hardwood were felled, and when the timber company had no further use for the land, they sold it and moved on. Only a few scrubby coppices and solitary parkland trees remain, and the Diana Plantation. This clump of trees surrounded a statue of the goddess of the hunt, Diana. She was mounted on a six foot plinth and was depicted holding a stag by the horns in order to plunge a dagger into its throat. Apparently Mark Rolle considered it bloodthirsty and unpleasant, but rather than have it removed — perhaps for a family or superstitious reasons — he surrounded it by trees. The trees remain, but the lead statue went during the War.

The ornamental lake remains, overgrown around its margins but the chain of fishponds have all but silted up. One of the favourite drives from the lake through the woods to Town Mills, some two miles distant on the River Torridge, is completely overgrown.

The woodland survived but is in different ownerships. Town Mills marked the termination of the Rolle Canal, built by Lord Rolle in

1823. It followed the course of the Torridge from Landcross enabling barges to reach Torrington from the Port of Bideford. The canal fell into disuse with the coming of the railway and few traces of it remain. No trace at all remains of the once fine yew walk from the house to the church at St. Giles. Called Church Walk a double line of yew trees extended from the eastern end of the terrace across the fields, but was felled for fear of cattle-poisoning.

Could it all have been saved?

Mark Rolle died without an heir — a common fault shared with his ancestors. The estate passed to his nephew Charles John Robert Hepburn Stuart Forbes Trefusis, 21st Baron Clinton. He already owned the vast Bicton lands and had no need of a large Victorian house in North Devon, and so began the chain of sales that led to the eventual destruction of Stevenstone.

After the Second World War there were hopes that a use could be found for the house as an isolation hospital, but nothing came of this and the once noble seat of the Rolles was allowed to fall into a gentle ruin.

ANNERY HOUSE

"Annery stands in a finely undulating park, richly wooded and forms a striking object from the road leading from Bideford to Torrington."

Thus was the house described in a guide to the County written towards the end of the nineteenth century. Less than a hundred years later it stood deserted and neglected, the parkland stripped of most of its timber, the house awaiting the final degradation. It was demolished in 1958.

Although the house was not old, built or rebuilt in 1800, the site was steeped in history and Annery was reputedly both haunted and accursed. The identity of the ghost was unknown and although no-one remembers the origin or reason for the curse, local rumour believed that no male would survive at Annery for more than one year. Only one male owner seems to have met with a sudden end, but the last two owners, both single, decided against taking up residence.

Annery was a Grade II listed building, though this made little difference when application was made to demolish the house. The official description of 1955 reads "The old house completely altered in 1800. Stucco front with Ionic order to full height and entablature plus parapet. On the east is a bow to full height. On the north is the projecting octagonal turret. Dilapidated. Historical connections with Chief Justice Hankford, 15th century. Passed to St. Leger family in 17th century.

Dower House, Grade III. Large Georgian stucco front, with parapet. Continuous Doric verandah."

The views from the house must have been magnificent for it occupied a superb position overlooking the wide valley of the River Torridge. Today most of the woodland has disappeared, modern outsize agricultural barns obtrude in the middle distance and a line of pylons marches aggressively down the hillside and across the valley. But the bungalow that somewhat cheekily squats on the site of Annery still enjoys good views, although unlike its predecessor, it does not make an inspiring object from the valley below.

The history of Annery is a long one. There are records that in the year 1260 Annery passed to the Stapledons, and Walter de Stapledon, Bishop of Exeter from 1307 to 1326 and Lord Treasurer to Edward II, was born there.

The various changes of ownership are not well documented, nor the changing fortunes that resulted in the house, by the end of the eighteenth century, being little better than a ruin. It would be logical to assume that at this time it changed hands and the new owners built the elegant stuccoed house around, or instead of, the older building. All that is left are some of the extensive outbuildings, built to such a high standard, so well designed and attractive to look at that one can only bemoan the loss of the house itself.

Regretfully, there are no existing pictures of Annery prior to the 1800 rebuilding, but the Rev. Richard Polwhele, writing at the end of the eighteenth century, described it as "a noble seat on the west-side of the Torridge over which it stands commanding a delightful prospect of the river. The house, now gone into decay, was heretofore stately and magnificent. It was famous for a large upper gallery in which might be placed 30 standing beds, 15 on each side and yet not one be seen there; nor could you from one bed see

Back view of Annery 1957

another. For the gallery being long and wainscotted, both to the right and left, there were several doors in that each led into little alcoves or apartments, large and convenient enough for private lodgings.''

Lyson, writing in 1822 in his Magna Britannia, also mentions the long gallery — a great rarity had it survived. He tells us that the house was modernised by the Tardrew family, who followed the Prusts and Johnsons as owners of the Estate, but pours cold water on the popularly believed story of the strange death of Annery's best known owner, Sir William Hankford, who has been suggested as the original Chief Justice in Shakespeare's Henry IV.

Hankford was created a Knight of the Bath at the coronation of Henry IV, made Chief Justice of the King's Bench ten days before the coronation of Henry V in 1413, and lived to see the accession of Henry VI. His death on 20th December, 1422 was popularly believed to have been caused by his own actions. He was shot by his own gamekeeper, whom he disturbed on a dark night after issuing instructions that anyone who did not reply when accosted should be shot. Lyson considers this much repeated tale suspicious and disbelieves the various reasons given for the apparent suicide, such as that Hankford was weary of life, worried about his future, or troubled by the affairs of the time. But until recent times, a venerable oak in the grounds was always known as Hankford's oak, under which the old judge was supposed to have met his end. His tomb is in the Annery aisle at Monkleigh Church.

The estate passed via the female line to the St. Leger family. Sir James St. Leger sold it to Tristram Arscott, whose descendant died in 1621 in possession of both Annery and nearby Half-Annery.

Although there are few photographs of Annery in its heyday, both interior and exterior were well documented before demolition. The architect is not known, but he designed a house that was apparently as delightful inside as it was out.

Auction particulars from 1912 have survived in the archives of the London estate agents, Knight, Frank and Rutley. They describe a compact and well thought out property, spacious but not vast. The portico, supported by Corinthian columns, had glass sides to protect the gentry from the weather. The outer hall, paved with stone and black marble, opened into a larger inner hall, some 26 feet by 16 feet. There were four reception rooms — the drawing room, 30 feet by 20 feet, a slightly smaller dining room with French casements and richly carved panelling, the library, 20 feet by 19 feet, and an oval room, 11 feet by 15 feet, with a bay window and wall recesses for statuary.

The domestic offices "well-screened from the Reception Rooms" contained a kitchen as large as the dining room with a back kitchen and scullery adjoining, and a butler's pantry, 16 feet by 9 feet, fitted with dresser, shelves, cupboards, sink and fireplace. "A separate lobby and corridor communicate with the Servant's Hall, 17 feet by 13 feet, with fireplace. In this room is the pull of the Call Bell and the clock case, and over this room is a Bed Room, Clock Tower and Bell Turret," The Servant's Hall must have been the octagon room and the servants were fortunate to have been allotted such a pleasant room with a commanding view straight down the main drive.

At the rear were well-equipped wine and beer cellars, a housekeeper's room, a bathroom and three W.C.'s. Upstairs, reached by a staircase of stone with a double flight of stairs guarded by a massive mahogany handrail and iron balusters and lit by a cupola, were six principal bedrooms, the oval boudoir with moulded ceiling and bay window, and two bathrooms. There were two additional staircases to six further bedrooms, the attic, two bathrooms and two W.C.'s. For a house built in 1800 to possess four bathrooms and five internal W.C.'s seems to indicate a commendable concern for cleanliness and hygiene unusual for the period.

The outbuildings were also somewhat unusual in that the stabling, coach-house and garage with motor-pit, apple room, wood house and two cider houses were in enclosed yards, partly glassed over, adjoining the rear of the main house. This civilised arrangement allowed the staff to go about their business in all weathers without getting wet and permitted the coachman and chauffeur to work unhindered on their vehicles. Other outbuildings included a larder, dairy salting house, wash-house and laundry, coal-house and cider cellar as well as the usual range of farm buildings. The same forethought went into the water supply. The property's own wells were augmented by a supply pumped by a Blake's

The staircase 1957

automatic ram from nearby Landcross Mill — up a very considerable hill — to a large reservoir at Beaconside, an adjoining property then in the same ownership, and thence by gravity to other large reservoirs at Annery. This, according to the particulars, "afforded a supply at high pressure for protection in case of Fire." This arrangement was still in operation in 1958.

The 1912 sale was occasioned by the death in her ninety sixth year of Mrs. Maria Somes. She was the widow of Joseph Somes of Blackwall who died in 1845. He was Member of Parliament for Dartmouth and at one time Governor of the New Zealand Company, and one of the largest ship owners of his day, and it was from his ship "The Tory" that Queen Victoria's sovereignty over New Zealand was declared. Mrs. Florence Westcott, born at the turn of the century, whose father was the estate carpenter, and has lived on the estate all her life, just remembers Mrs. Somes. She gives a fascinating glimpse of life in a large house in the closing years of the Edwardian era.

As a child, she played in the grounds with Henry, the coachman's son, dressed smartly in case the gentry should see them. She remembers the garden parties when she and Henry hid behind the laurel hedge to watch the grand ladies in beautiful dresses with their parasols. "But even better was when my father came home. He used to have to help out, wearing his best boots and trousers with a clean white apron for the occasion. He always came home with plenty of left-over food and ginger ale galore, and we would imagine we were the gentry, eating the same food."

"We used to have such beautiful weather in those days — long hot summers. We would go down to watch the men harvesting — all the men servants stopped their usual work to help get in the hay — and we children would make sure we were there when tea was sent down from the house."

Food seems to have played an important part in the life of those far off days, especially when seen through the eyes of a child. To Florence, Christmas meant a party in the big house. "So many of the workmen went in for dinner and we would have lots of food and the butler would bring in a huge round pudding with brandy burning on it and a sprig of holly." Another party was given on Guy Fawkes night when everyone gathered round a huge bonfire and there would be plenty of fireworks to delight a child.

The Annery estate meant employment and security for many of

The staff outing.

the local people. In Mrs. Somes' day there were 2 housemaids, 2 kitchen maids, a cook and kitchen boy, 2 ladies maids, 2 footmen and a butler. Outside staff included a coachman and groom, 4 gardeners, a carpenter, a mason and a stableboy. The head gardener lived in the Dower House, or Bungalow as it was then called. This attractive Georgian house with six bedrooms, drawing room and dining room, kitchens and sculleries and its own range of outbuildings and stabling was a very grand gardener's cottage, and today is a most desirable residence. The other estate workers were housed in the four lodges and the cottages at Annery Kiln on the River Torridge. Mrs. Westcott remembers Mid Lodge with particular affection for it was her childhood home.

"Mid Lodge drive was very sweet. As you left the house it entered a dense wood and went down the hill between big mossy banks. Across the road at the bottom was an ornamental gate in the hedge giving on to the railway line. Mrs. Somes had a flight of steps built and a small platform so that one of the footmen could wait for the train which slowed down at this point to pass the newspapers to him." No sign remains of either the gate or platform and even the drive has disappeared since the lodge passed into private

Panelled Dining Room 1957

The Oval Room 1957

The Drawing Room 1957

ownership. The newest lodge is North Lodge, built in the early 1900's at the entrance to the new drive, cut by Mrs. Somes to enable her to reach Landcross and its church. A guidebook of 1894 describes the drive as being new, and keeping a picturesque and nearly level course following the windings of the hill until it opened by a deep cutting, driven through solid rock onto the highway between Bideford and Torrington.

The estate lands were divided between the parishes of Monkleigh and Landcross and Mrs. Somes went regularly to the two churches. At the end of her life she travelled to Landcross in a wheelchair. Mrs. Westcott remembers the seats set at intervals along the drive to enable the footmen who pushed her to have a rest.

The estate in those days was run in the true country house manner. "There were glasshouses with peaches, nectarines, ferns, flowers — everything you could think of. Beautiful flower beds, and every Saturday four men would rake the gravel on the front drive. Life was so different then — everyone took such pride in what they did, how they dressed, their homes, no matter how poor they were. And although it was a poor time generally, we were not aware of it because we were all looked after so well by the estate. It was a happy time and a happy house in Mrs. Somes' days."

The next owners were Mr. and Mrs. Bayly. They modernized the house and installed an electricity plant. But within a matter of weeks of moving in Mr. Bayly, a great polo player, died of meningitis. His widow continued to live at Annery until 1921. She planted many beautiful shrubs in the grounds, and also created a Japanese garden near the top of the Mid Lodge drive, with a wooden bridge, ornaments, storks and Japanese shrubs. Only clumps of bamboo have survived. Before she sold the estate, Mrs. Bayly offered all her tenants the chance to buy their cottage or farm, with the exception of the lodges and Home Farm.

Annery was bought by a Miss Lilias Fleming, who lived there with her adopted daughter, Crystal Frazer. Miss Fleming died in 1941 aged 86. She was the last person to live in Annery and after her death a sale was held of all her possessions. No-one remembers if a

The Electricity Plant

demolition sale was ever held, but at some time between Miss Fleming's death and 1957, many of the fittings were taken away from Annery. It was reputedly beautifully appointed, with marble fireplaces, and chandeliers in many of the ground floor rooms. Several of them were panelled, the dining room with ornate carved walnut panelling, possibly French, and the ceiling was decorated with ornamental plasterwork panels. One room was hung with blue silk and in the oval boudoir everything was curved, from the domed ceiling to the pink marble fireplace.

The estate, with nearly 100 acres of woodland and its "finely timbered parkland" was bought by a Mr. Green, a timber merchant from the North of England. Yet again it was the trees that were responsible for the loss of the house. When the estate was sold in September 1958, following his death, it had been reduced from 422 acres in Mrs. Somes' time to 175 acres of which only some 20 acres and three small plantations were woodland.

Whether he believed in the old superstition or simply found Annery too large for a man living on his own, Mr. Green never moved into the house, living at the Dower House on his visits to the estate, leaving Annery locked up.

Mr. Green was friendly with Mrs. Westcott and gave her a key to the old house so that she could visit it and keep an eye on things when he was away. She had heard the story of the ghost, but never believed it until her dog refused to go past the entrance of the octagon room and, trembling and with bristles up, had to be carried. The ghost was supposedly of a lady in crinoline with a poke bonnet and was seen on one occasion by the local policeman. In Mrs. Somes' time two of the servants heard the piano playing in the octagon room when everyone in the house had gone to church.

The estate was split into ten lots, unless sold as one. Lot 3, the Mansion House and lawns, were sold prior to the auction to a Mr. Berridge. He was the last owner of Annery House and lost no time in pulling it down. He built the bungalow on the site and sold it to the daughter of the new owners of the Dower House. After surviving a near-fatal road accident, he, like the house he had so recently demolished, disappeared.

DUNSLAND

An early drawing c. 1716

This chapter in many ways tells the saddest story, for Dunsland House, unlike the others in this book, was not deliberately destroyed. A noble and beautiful property, it was reduced within the space of a few short hours to a ruined, blackened shell. Fire swept through the old building in the early hours of 18th November, 1967, and by dawn it was apparent that Dunsland's century's long history was over. Nothing was left but smoking walls and piles of charred timbers and smouldering debris. It could never be rebuilt.

Dunsland House, together with 92 acres of surrounding farmland, had been purchased by the National Trust in 1954 with a bequest. At the time it was intended to find a suitable tenant with complete restoration left to a later date. The exterior of the house, then in very poor shape, was immediately put in order with a £30,000 grant from the Ministry of Public Buildings and Works and the house was furnished with surplus from other Trust Properties including Saltram, Polesden Lacey, Stourhead, Arlington, Killerton and Prattshayes.

The house was let and until the early 1960's was left untouched. The public were admitted, but only on a few days each week and were shown round by the tenants, Mrs. Enid Caffyn and her son, John Price.

But prior to that disastrous November night, Dunsland had been the subject of an extensive restoration scheme, not entirely completed even then. After the long years of neglect the house had been completely restored, redecorated and sumptuously furnished. A local building firm employing a team of over ten skilled craftsmen were just coming to the end of two years of meticulous work. New lintels had been inserted above all the windows; flooring had been taken up, the timbers treated and repaired and the boards replaced; much of the panelling had similarly been removed and replaced; pegs holding the plaster ceilings in place had been repaired; doors had been unhinged and taken ouside so that old paint could be burnt off without fire risk; dry rot had been eradicated. The house had been redecorated from top to bottom with old-fashioned lead-based paints, and a new custodian's flat incorporated on the first floor. Only the front porch was uncompleted and the work was scheduled to start the Monday following the fire.

The Trust had not stinted either money or expertise and it is probable that Dunsland had never before been so finely bedecked. As well as the Trust's own furnishings, the house contained many treasures on loan from private owners, such as the set of nine Chippendale chairs lent by the conductor, Sir Adrian Boult and embroidered by his sister.

But before the grand opening, all was lost.

The value of the contents was put at £100,000 and despite contemporary newspaper reports to the contrary, they were not insured. The house itself was insured only against minimal damage. The Trust do not insure their properties against total destruction, considering it pointless to rebuild, thus creating a twentieth century sham. Once a house has gone, it has gone forever.

The cause of the fire was never established. What is certain is that once started, it spread with horrifying rapidity until the whole house was ablaze from end to end. The custodian and his mother were roused by the barking of their sheepdog and had time only to dress hurriedly before making their escape down the main staircase. Their flat had no separate fire escape.

Fire engines from three local stations, Holsworthy, Hatherleigh

7.30 a.m. 18th November, 1967

and Torrington fought the blaze for many hours but, as one of them put it, they could do little except put on a show. The firemen remember it as one of the largest and most spectacular fires they had witnessed. One of the Torrington men described that night. "As we approached, Dunsland could be seen, one mass of flames. It was tragic. All the beautiful furniture inside was lit up by the fire, but we could not get in, and had to watch it slowly being destroyed. It was a very clear, cold night — but not where we were — the heat was intense. After the fire, when we were searching amongst the rubble to see if there was anything at all that could be salvaged, we narrowly escaped injury when one of the huge chimney stacks suddenly collapsed. There was nothing left to salvage, but I do remember the irony of seeing in the cellars a great pile of fire extinguishers. Apparently the custodian had been a salesman in that line." That same fireman also remembers that as they left many weary hours later, they met a van at the entrace gate. The driver had come to refix some slates.

The fire had devastated Dunsland so completely that the walls were pronounced unsafe and a decision had to be made speedily before someone was hurt by falling masonry. Dunsland was bulldozed, the rubble filling up the cellars thus destroying all that was left. The wine cellars, the six huge granite troughs used for salt meat, the brewing vats, all were buried, the site levelled and a commemorative plaque let into what was one of the courtyard walls. Would the Arscotts and Bickfords who owned the estate for so long, consider it the final indignity that Dunsland is now a caravan club site?

For me the loss was personal, for Dunsland was a house I knew well and at which I was a frequent guest. Memories come flooding back — of the evening sun lighting up the warm stone, of the splendid view from the leads high above the courtyard, of the huge timbers in the roof, of sitting in front of a roaring log fire in the Justice Room and not minding the draughts, and of evenings when the house was filled with music lovers listening to a string quartet or a recital — and of that terrible Monday morning when I came down the drive and saw the chimneys and roofless walls stark against a clear blue sky.

It is hard to make an objective appraisal without nostalgia creeping in. For Dunsland was a very beautiful house. There was no other quite like it in North Devon — it was a Grade 1 listed building — and its loss was therefore the greater. Part of its charm lay in the total unexpectedness of the visitor's first view of the house. There were no impressive entrance gates, no lodges, no hint at all that the drive led to anything other than a farm. Most people probably anticipated a glorified Devon farmhouse and instead were confronted, after crossing a field or two, with the magnificence of the North front, looking out across the valley. The setting was admirable, on rising ground, yet sheltered by woodland to the rear. Perhaps it looked somewhat incongruous amidst rural farmland, but Dunsland was a truly "stately" home.

The records of ownership are incomplete but it seems certain that Dunsland passed in unbroken line down the long centuries from the days of William the Conqueror until it was sold in 1947. The date of the first house is not known but the Manor of Dunsland is mentioned in Domesday as belonging to John Cadiho. The name crops up intermittently and is last mentioned in 1428 when the male line apparently died out and John Dabernon, husband of Thomasine

Dunsland — an old print

Cadiho, inherited. The Dabernon ownership was short-lived and two generations later John's grand-daughter, Elizabeth took the estate to her husband's family, the Battyns.

At this time the original house would almost certainly have resembled many small manor houses of the time, with an open-ceilinged hall and kitchens. Until the 1950's this wing survived, running back at right angles from the south end of the east wing. It is described in the National Trust booklet as being of rubble walls, some four to five feet thick, with stone quoins to the small windows, which were mullioned and heavily barred. The door from the courtyard entered a simple screens passage separating what would have been the hall and kitchen but became the kitchen and back kitchen when later additions to the house were made. The floors were of slate and in the kitchen was a huge fireplace with a granite lintel. The ceiling beams were studded with massive iron hooks as were the chimneys, for smoking pork, and in the back kitchen was a "cloam" oven where all the houshold bread was baked as late as

1939. The staircase walls and ceiling were lined with oak panelling as were part of the bedrooms, all of which led out of each other. The main bedroom had become the housekeeper's room and one wall was lined with an enormous cupboard containing over 100 small drawers. The East or Jacobean wing was the first extension to Dunsland and extended as far as the front porch. The roof of this wing was described by Arthur Oswald in Country Life (July 1960) as typical of the fifteenth century or, at the latest, early Tudor.

". . . the doorway is not likely to be much before 1550 and may be Elizabethan. The porch gives entrance to a screens passage with the hall (in recent times called the Justice Room) opening off to the left. The hall was remodelled after the Restoration and has a flat ceiling with a room above that represents an earlier arrangement when, quite possibly, there was a high hall going up to the roof. At the end of the hall is a narrow room with a five-light mullioned window and a decorated ceiling having curved and intersecting ribbing forming heart-shaped patterns. As the thistle occurs among the ornaments it may be dated in James I's reign, after the union of the crowns.

The barrel roof

The room above this parlour has a barrel ceiling . . . with a geometrical pattern of broad bands decorated with designs of fruit and foliage and with an elaborate frieze with stooping figures at intervals carrying the cornice on their head and shoulders . . . it is dated 1660. That it is an insertion can be seen by going up into the attic where one finds above it the remains of a much older roof with arch-braced principals and curved wind-braces . . ."

In 1522 John Arscott inherited Dunsland on the death of his wife Phillipa's father. The Arscotts were an old-established Holsworthy family and continued in ownership for over a century and a half. The second John Arscott who inherited on the death of his father in 1580, married Mary Monk, great aunt of the General Monk of Royalist fame who led the Restoration. Four houses within a dozen miles of each other were built or enlarged as a result of connections with General Monk and the Royalist cause. The General was born at the family home of Potheridge on the River Torridge, and he was still building Great Potheridge at the time of his death. Tetcott near Holsworthy was another Arscott home much enlarged, as was Dunsland itself. Stowe on the North Cornish coast was the home of the Grenville Family, created Earls of Bath, who built themselves a huge mansion in keeping with their rise to fortune. None of the four houses survives, although parts of Tescott remain.

The last Arscott to succeed was Arthur, John and Mary's son, in 1623. His daughter Grace, widow of William Bickford, inherited in 1662 and kept her son, another Arscott, waiting until 1686 when she died in her 86th year. Mother and son were responsible for much improvement and enlarging and when Arscott Bickford died in 1693 the Dunsland he left was basically that which survived until 1967. His mother, Grace Bickford, greatly embellished the old house but stopped short of adding to it. This was left to her son who transformed Dunsland from a small manor house to a grand mansion by building the North or Restoration wing. Built of stone faced with ashlar and fronted with a series of terraces, it was this wing that gave Dunsland its imposing appearance from across the valley. There were several fine rooms — a central salon, drawing room, library and parlour. With the exception of the drawing room, these were plainly decorated with ceilings of simple moulded panels. The panelling to the walls was either painted or stained to resemble walnut.

But the drawing room was indeed an exception and it seems

The Drawing Room

certain that Arscott spared no expense in the decoration of this room, employing the finest craftsmen in the country. The room was beautifully proportioned with windows on two sides and although the decoration was profuse the room was not oppressive or "overdone." The chimneypiece was exquisitely carved after the style of Grinling Gibbons with cherubs, game birds, fruit and flowers. The coving to the ceiling was decorated with a continuous chain of swagged garlands and the ceiling itself was magnificent. A central garland of flowers was surrounded by decorated panels, sprays of foliage, panels of military trophies and circlets. The plasterer used strips of wire or copper suspended from the ceiling round which he created his flowers and foliage. The workmanship was so delicate that one expected the slightest breeze to set the flowers trembling.

Whether the family fortunes declined after Arscott's death in 1693, or whether future owners preferred living elswhere, the house escaped the alterations and "improvements" imposed on many large houses by successive generations, and survived, dilapidated but almost intact, until the restoration work began.

Arscott was followed by the eldest son of his third wife, William. His son, another Arscott, inherited in 1740, and his brother George in 1771. George's son, the third Arscott, was apparently a gambler who, by the time he died in 1812, had wasted much of his substance. His sister, Mary Bickford, wife of William Holland Coham, was the next owner. Two more William Cohams inherited, the second dying in 1880. The estate then passed via his sister Augusta, married to Major Harvey Dickinson who died at an early age in 1901, to their son Arscott Harvey Dickinson. He was the 29th owner in unbroken line and it was he who in 1947 put Dunsland up for sale.

Dunsland had never been his home until latter years. Although he and his sons had tried valiantly to maintain the family property, two World Wars, shortage of staff and shortage of money caused him to give up the unequal struggle.

The sale particulars, dated 26th November, 1947 describe the house as being in need of considerable repair and redecoration. Years of neglect by both owners and tenants had taken their toll, for Dunsland appears not to have been occupied fully by its owners for some time. Lyson in 1822 describes the house as being "occasionally occupied by the Reverend W. Holland Coham" and Kelly's directory of 1910 states that although owned by Arscott Dickinson, the "house was the residence of William Clifton-Mogg."

The Estate was offered for sale in 29 lots.

Lot 1 was the house itself with parkland and woodlands totalling 91 acres. The ground floor had six reception rooms, including the Justice Hall then used as a billiard room, the hall, and commodious domestic offices. The first floor contained 13 bedrooms with five more bedrooms above.

There was a range of two garages, stabling for five, saddle and grooms rooms, laundry room, brick and timber granary and two other stores.

Water was from wells near the house by semi-rotary pump and drainage was to the larger fish pond.

The kitchen garden, then as now, was described as overgrown but capable of being turned into a profitable market garden.

Other lots included the Bickford Arms, 6 dairy farms and extensive and valuable woodland. The schedule of trees listed 306 oak, 3 turkey oaks, 581 beech, 10 Spanish chestnuts, and 34 horse

Dunsland — before the fire

chestnuts, 43 lime, 1 walnut, 1 Wellingtonia, 2 monkey puzzle, 15 spruce, 24 silver spruce, 33 Scotch fir, 12 larch, 3 cedar and numerous sycamore, ash, alder and elm.

The house and much of the woodland were sold to a Mr. De Savoury from London, whose main interest was the "valuable timber" and without the valiant gesture of Mr. Philip Tilden, the house itself would have suffered the same fate as Eggesford and Stevenstone. Ironically this course of events may well have resulted in at least a ruinous Dunsland remaining for the benefit of historians and romantics.

Philip Tilden was an architect who loved old houses and had already restored nearby Wortham Manor. He described his first visit to Dunsland in 1949 on behalf of the County Planning Authority when he found the house in a very bad state. "Two great slate tanks had been fitted at some time above the main staircase to collect rain-water from the roof. The bottom had fallen out of one of them and whenever it rained all the water from the roof cascaded down the stairs. The magnificent drawing room ceiling was on the

The Justice Room

point of collapse owing to a rotting beam. A timber merchant had bought the estate and was cutting down the fine trees. "In spite of my report nobody bothered about the place and my wife and I felt we had no alternative but to buy it ourselves . . . We did emergency repairs to keep out the weather, paid the timber merchant five pounds for every tree he left standing, fitted a small kitchen into one corner of the hall with two bathrooms over, and moved in." Despite failing health, Tilden arrested the decay and began to restore the house. But he died in 1954 and his widow offered the property to the National Trust.

Inexplicably, unless he felt the house large enough to cope with, Philip Tilden removed the roof from the original house, the kitchen wing, and by the time the Trust took possession, it had gone beyond reclaim and was demolished.

Now the house has suffered the same fate and the only reminders of all that long history are names. Dunsland Station, a halt on the defunct Halwill to Bude line, survives as a place name and Dunsland Cross on the main road between Holsworthy and Hatherleigh, marks the emergence of the back drive. The families are remembered at the nearby Bickford Arms and the Arscott Arms public houses.

Dunsland from the North showing granary, courtyard area and position of former kitchen wing

YEO VALE

Few houses could have a stranger or more tragic ending to a long history than Yeo Vale House at Alwington, a small parish on the North Devon coast. The house that died of pique, is how one local newspaper put it, and with justification.

The squat, unpretentious Devon manor house with a history going back to at least the fifteenth century was literally abandoned and left to die. The owner, Stephen Berrold, turned the key in the lock one morning in 1938, drove off and apparently never gave the house another thought.

It stood for many years, deserted and empty, gazing forlornly out across the fields, like a dog patiently waiting for its master to return. But he never did. Gradually the air of decay and desolation became more marked until its eventual demolition became only a matter of time. But to this day the piece of land on which the house once stood still belongs to the heirs of Stephen Berrold, and presumably it always will.

The house itself was a low, rambling building with a tower-like entrance porch and gothic windows. It was of moderate size, more of an enlarged farmhouse than a manor house and would have made a delightful home or small hotel. The situation, facing down the valley of the River Yeo, was warm and sheltered. The now-levelled site blends with the pasture that was once parkland, and the only clue offered to the passerby of the house's former existence is the wrought iron gates set in the boundary wall.

Piecing together the true reasons for Stephen Berrold's extraordinary action is not easy. The man was something of a mystery and many conflicting stories have grown up over the years. There was a quarrel, it seems certain, and it concerned the trees around the house.

When Berrold bought Yeo Vale he would very much have liked the land around it, and in particular the woodland as he was fond of trees and loved to walk amongst them. He apparently came to an arrangement with Farmer John Westaway that he would pay £30 a year for the use of the woods and that no trees would be felled without prior discussion. All went well for a number of years. Mr. Berrold laid out a walk in the woods and the farm supplied the big house with dairy produce. The row came when Mr. Berrold returned from one of his frequent absences to find Mr. Westaway had been to work with his axe. Whether Mr. Berrold lost his temper because the trees had been felled, or because he hadn't been consulted, isn't clear.

Whatever the true facts or causes, the result was out of all proportion. He would leave Yeo Vale House, Stephen Berrold announced, and no-one else would ever live in it again. The Westaways would not only lose a valuable customer for all time, for a neighbour they would have a dark and empty house.

So what kind of man was he that could go off and leave his home to rot?

Stephen Berrold emerges as a strange, shadowy figure, possibly part foreign, described as the local mystery-man, with strange coming and goings and "dark people" to wait on him. Some people thought he was a foreign spy, others a Secret Service Agent. Very few people in the parish now remember him, but Mr. Frank Daniels who worked at Yeo Vale as a gardener swept away much of the rumour and hearsay. "He was always a gentleman to us," said Mr. Daniels, "But I didn't know no more about him on the last day than

The Front Door

I did on the first."

According to Mr. Daniels, the Berrolds moved into Yeo Vale around 1928. He had been in Palestine and brought with him his wife and three foreign servants, a Persian chauffeur, and two girls, one Muslim, one Arab. The chauffeur stayed, but the girls were soon off, not finding Alwington and the damp North Devon climate to their liking.

From what people remember, it seems clear that Stephen Berrold was, to say the least, an unusual man, if not an eccentric one. He did not like to be questioned and could not bear to be crossed. His wife was said to be terrified of him. He was a man given to taking long solitary walks, often at night, and both Mr. Daniels and his wife Amy remember lights burning far into the night in Berrold's room.

But they never did find out what his business was or where his money came from. He had an office in London and every so often would disappear for a month at a time. Parcels would arrive from abroad, often from India, but Mr. Daniels never had any idea what

Mr. Berrold was "about". Considering that Mrs. Daniels worked in the house as a cleaner, and Mr. Daniels was obviously a valued servant, one of several who went with the Berrold household when they moved, it seems strange that during those nine or ten years neither of them ever got so much of a hint of their employer's occupation or where his apparently unlimited money came from.

Certainly they remember him as being very open-handed with his staff and the village folk. Every Christmas Amy Daniels made out a list of the children, each one of whom received a toy. A huge Christmas tree decorated one of the main rooms in the house and all the village folk would be asked down for a party, with more presents all round. And on Guy Fawkes night Mr. Berrold really went to town with a huge display on the lawn in front of the house which would take the staff all day to set up in readiness for the evening's party.

But he didn't mix with the gentry. Morning callers received short shrift from Stephen Berrold and he never repaid their visits. For some reason he had no wish to mix with the neighbours of his own standing and no desire to become part of the social life of the area.

To the people of North Devon, accustomed as they then were to staying all their lives in one place and treating a visit to the neighbouring market town as a major expedition, Berrold must have seemed something of a mystery. And he had an aeroplane! He kept his own monoplane at Stibb Cross, some few miles away and used this for journeys to and from London. Mr. Daniels remembers being taken up in it along with other members of the staff — an experience he looks back on with mixed feelings. Plane-owning tycoons are something of a rarity today, but before the Second World War were virtually unheard of.

Once the decision had been made to leave Yeo Vale, despite the pleas of Mrs. Berrold who liked the house, the Daniels had to decide whether they would go with them, or stay at home. Mrs. Daniels' objections because of her aged mother were put aside by Mr. Berrold who said that he would fly her back whenever she wanted to come. So together they left Yeo Vale and moved to the new home, Stodden Park, near Petersfield in Hampshire. But the Daniels' exile was not for long. After only a few months, Mrs. Berrold died suddenly. She was in her early sixties, and apparently the shock to Stephen Berrold was severe. Even for this strange man his grief-stricken behaviour was bizarre. He had all her clothes packed into her Buick car which he then ordered the chauffeur to drive over the edge of the cliffs. Not surprisingly, the chauffeur refused, so Berrold had a large pit dug in the grounds of Stodden Park, set fire to the car and its contents and buried the remains. The ashes of his dead wife he kept by him, even placing them on the pillow beside him at night. However, he didn't die of his grief, but found consolation by marrying a French lady, and the last the Daniels heard of him he had gone to live in Africa.

Yeo Vale house was designated a Grade II Listed Building in 1955 and the official description was of an 18th century building, faced with stucco, of two storeys with a hipped slate roof, and seven sash windows with pointed Gothic glazing bars. The central portion was described as the castellated 15th century gatehouse of a 15th century mansion. A footnote reads "Interior is said to have been gutted and empty 12 years. All land sold. Dry rot."

It has been described as a Georgian rebuild of a big mediaeval mansion in the Picturesque style, an apt description for it was attractive even in decay. The original house must have been very old because there is evidence that the chapel existed in the fourteenth century. It was licensed in 1375 and again in 1406. This chapel was originally close to the house but at some time was moved across the road, when and for what reason is not clear, to its present site amongst the trees. The north transept, north door and south aisle were easily recognizable 40 years ago, but alas this is so no longer. Today it is difficult to distinguish the ruins. For many years it had been used as a shippon, the walls pulled down where they were dangerous, and altered to make a more serviceable structure. Nettles, brambles and ivy have joined with the weather and cattle to hasten its decay and before long the chapel in the trees will be a fast-fading memory.

It was said to contain many inscriptions to the Gifford family, one time owners of Yeo Vale and this could explain the absence of memorials to owners of the house in the parish church at Alwington. Only the later owners, the Morrison and Kirkwood families, are commemorated there. The Morrisons bought the house in 1739 from the Brutons, owners since the late 1600's, and it descended through the female line to Major James Morrison Kirkwood, who died in 1907.

There is virtually no documentation of the architectural history of Yeo Vale. One source states that parts dated from 1260. The oldest

The End

existing portion would have been the central stone tower and entrance porch. One theory is that this was all that was left of an ancient priory, but there is no evidence to substantiate this. The chapel cannot be taken as proof as many large houses in remote areas had their own chapel — it was more convenient and saved having to transport the entire household to the parish church every Sunday.

Pictures of the house when lived in seem non-existent, and only a few remain of it in decay. Of the interior there are no records except the memories of someone who used to wander there as a small boy. He remembers the entrance porch had a beamed ceiling, with bosses at the intersections. A narrow passage ran back into the house with two deeply recessed doorways. That on the left entered into the 'L' shaped drawing room. This doorway and its surrounding panelling were mahogany on the passage side but far more exotic on the inner side. The door, panelling and door linings were painted black and heavily decorated in gold. They were salvaged from the house and

Mr and Mrs Berrold

The Staircase

can be seen at Lenwood House, near Bideford. A matching dummy door, similarly painted, balanced the first, but this has vanished. There was an ornate marble fireplace and an unusual plasterwork coving of acanthus leaves behind curved ribbing. On the right of the passage was the dining room with a vaulted ceiling. Ribs from the four corners ran diagonally into the centre where they met in a large and very ornate central boss. The walls and floors were of pine and both doors had carved pediments. There was a room that had been a library, but everything — bookcases, fireplace, even floorboards, had already been removed. This room had a false window, the end window of the principal front.

At the end of the central passageway was the staircase, a door on the left leading to the servants' quarters and kitchens, and on the right a passage led to the dining room and to a study. This was a small, dark room built against the hillside where the small boy, to his joy, discovered a secret panel opening into the wine cellar!

The mahogany staircase rose in a dog-leg lit by a large Palladian window with mahogany pillars and panelling.

An unusual feature was an internal conservatory with a glass roof but no windows. It was bounded by the dining room passage and the billiard room, which was probably a later addition at the back of the house. Although the attractive gothic windows on the principal front matched, nothing else did. Those to the right of the tower, the dining room and false library windows were shorter and the rooms obviously lower than the drawing room. The roof was also lower, and this would explain the strange differences in floor levels of the bedrooms. Those over the drawing room each had their own flight of steps because they were at a higher level than the central passage.

Yeo Vale's end was ignominious. For many years it was used as a handy farm building. The gothic windows were taken out to enable bales of hay and bags of fertilizer to be lifted up on a conveyor belt and stored in the bedrooms. Calves were reared in the kitchen, pigs in the old library, and poultry kept upstairs. Mr. Norman Westaway, son of the farmer who fell out with Stephen Berrold, found that despite its usefulness, the old building was becoming yearly more of a liability. The former stables had been converted into their farmhouse in 1962, with only a three foot gap between them and the back of the derelict house, a gap that the rats jumped easily. One chimney had blown down in a gale, the floors and

First floor — steps to bedrooms

Yeo Vale 1972. The Westaway's farmhouse in on the left

ceilings were rotten, local children used it as an adventure playground and their older brothers and sisters went there for an illicit smoke. Before long Mr. Westaway could forsee a serious accident and no-one was surprised when he applied for permission to demolish the house. What alternative was there for a house abandoned by its owner?

Before demolishing a property he did not own, Mr. Westaway took out an insurance policy and published notices of his intention, but no-one objected or stepped forward to claim the property.

The end came in 1973 when it was bulldozed into a heap of rubble, and the site levelled.

All that remains are the converted stables, the former leanto now used for table-tennis, the ruined kennels where Berrold kept his greyhounds, the walled garden, and the weir in the river that Berrold used to generate electricity.

The ornate but rusting wrought iron gates stand a silent witness and monument to one man's folly that could bring so many years of history to such a sorry end.

WINSCOTT HOUSE

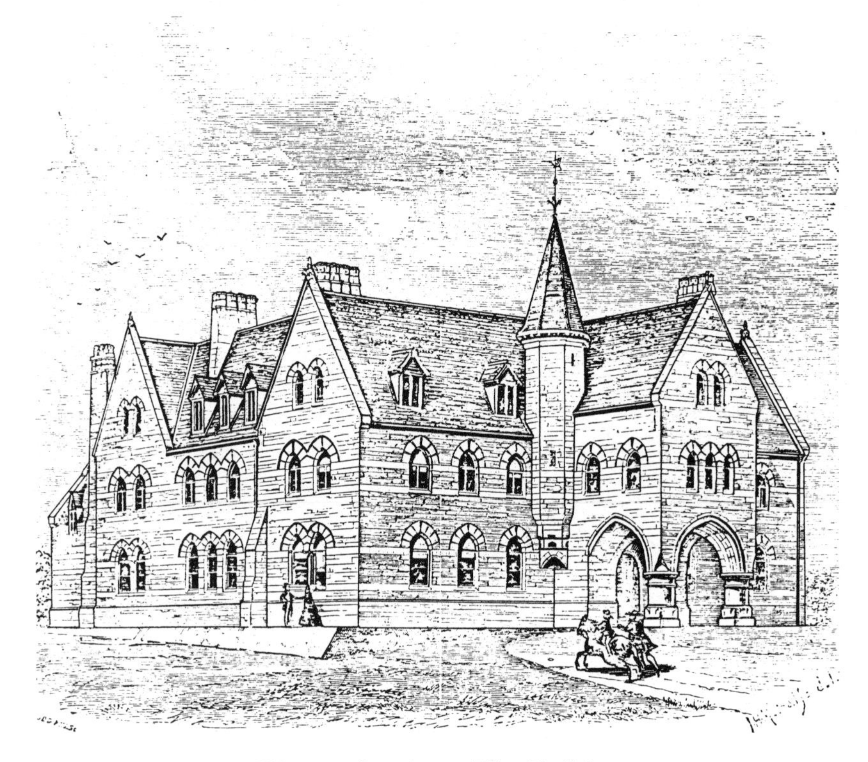

Illustration from *The Builder*

In a remote parish in the middle of Devon there stood for less than 100 years a large Victorian house. Winscott House at Petersmarland, built in 1865, was occupied for little more than 50 years. Few now remember it and all signs of its existence have disappeared save for the lodge and the imposing entrance gates.

For many centuries a house had stood at Winscott, the home of the Stevens family, whose name was prominent in the history of the nearby market town of Torrington and who also owned Cross, a large mansion on the outskirts of that town. The fate of the original house is uncertain — either it fell a victim to fire or to the Victorian passion for tearing down the old and erecting more lavishly in the new style.

In October 1865, when designs of the new house were published in The Builder magazine, the owner was given as Mr. J.C. Moore-Stevens, son of the late Archdeacon Moore-Stevens of Exeter. The architect was Mr. William White and the house was built entirely of the local brick, quarried at the nearby Marland clay works. Known as Marland brick, its yellow colour was quite distinctive and can be seen in many buildings in the North Devon area.

The house was large, basically 100 feet square, with servants' quarters added to the rear. The plans show a typically Victorian layout with over half the floor space allotted to domestic offices. The central hall was nearly 30 feet square, open to the roof, and finished with a lantern. An arcaded gallery connected this with the porch below and above. Drawing room and dining room were both about 30 by 20 feet. Mr. Moore-Stevens would appear to have been a local magistrate, for Winscott incorporated a Justice Room, accessible from the rear and with its own waiting lobby. The front porch was a massive affair, vaulted in brick, with supporting "monoliths of granite". Above was a boudoir and above again, as far away as possible, and approached only by a turret stair, was the smoking room.

The Builder states that the cost of the building was over £7,000 and that the proprietor had, at his own expense, rebuilt the parish church.

Local people still remember the last owner of Winscott, Col. Richard Arthur Moore-Stevens, born in 1854. He was a deeply religious man, who walked to church each Sunday rather than put his coachman and grooms to work on the seventh day. Winscott might still have been standing today had not his son fallen in love with, and married a Catholic. Apparently this so incensed the Colonel that he disinherited him and this may have been a contributory factor to the family deserting Winscott.

Around 1920 the house was shut up and the Moore-Stevens moved to Exeter. Col. Moore Stevens died in March, 1931, and both he and his wife, May Clare Sophy who died the previous year, are buried in the churchyard at Petersmarland.

Inside the church is a prominent memorial to Richard Stevens, who died in 1776, and to his wife Elizabeth who died in 1760. Sadly it also commemorates four of their children who died aged 16, 19, 29 and 31. A daughter, Elizabeth, has her own memorial — she married John Clevland, MP for Banstaple, and died in 1792. J.C. Moore-

Stevens erected a memorial window to his two infant daughters who died in 1856 and 1861, and a second window to another daughter who died in 1868 four days after her seventeenth birthday.

After the death of Col. Moore-Stevens, Winscott was sold. Following the usual pattern of the time, a timber merchant bought the grounds and a firm of builders, Chambers of Winkleigh, became eventual owners of the empty house. It seems to have been something of a sleeping beauty, for few of the neighbouring population remember its exact end, but talk of gradual demolition and decay. The army rejected the house as unfit for troops because some of the roof had been removed. Material from the house supposedly went towards building a local village hall.

But at some stage it was finally demolished and the land sold to a local farmer. He remembers huge cellars under the house and a large range of stables, barns and farm buildings. Two wells, one over 60 feet deep and one even deeper, were both filled in as a danger to children and livestock.

The hard tennis court has vanished, along with the orchard, the terraces and walled gardens. A few of the beautiful trees and shrubs that graced the parkland remain and a curiously level area in the middle of a green field, the site of Winscott House.

Plans as printed in *The Builder*

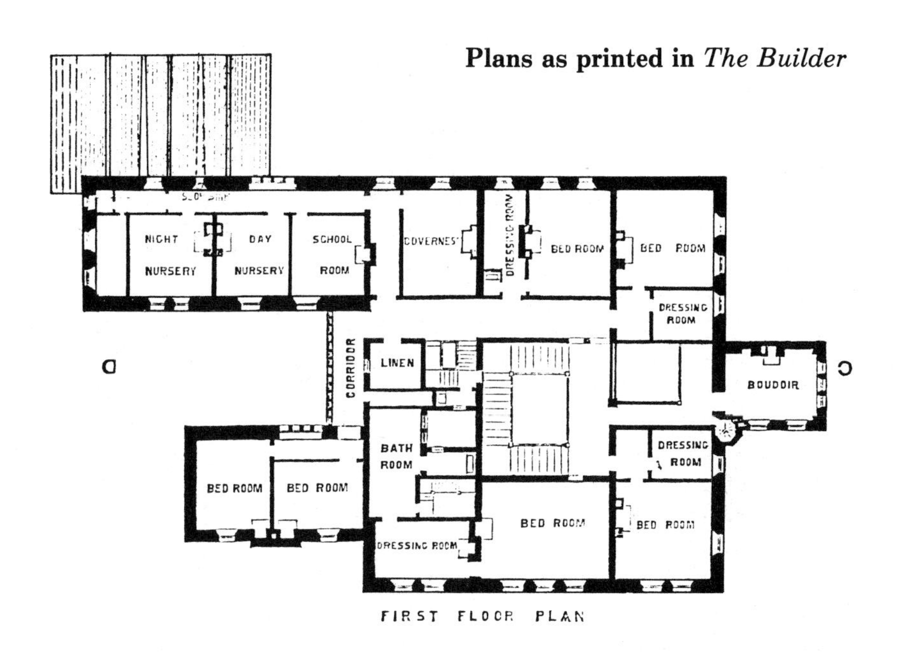

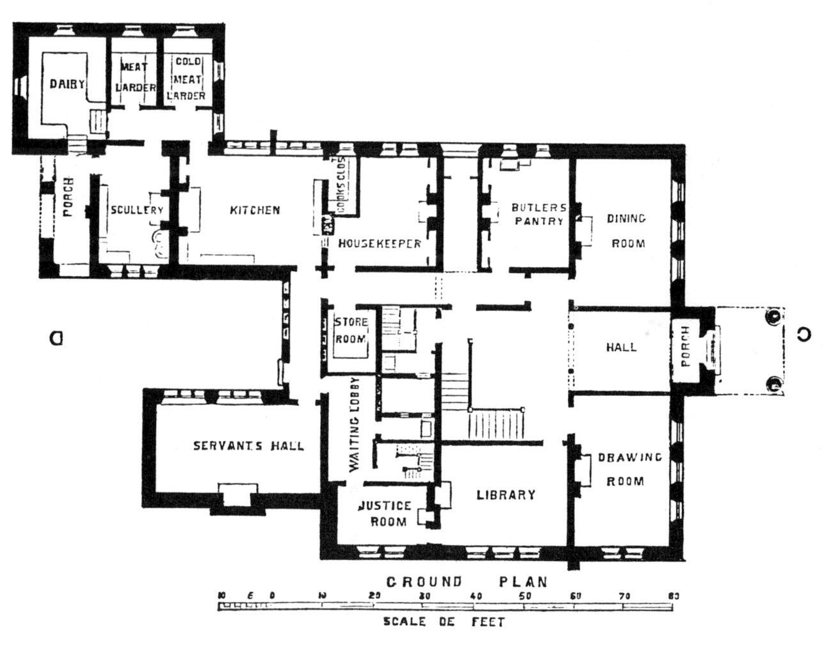

EGGESFORD

The former home of the Earls of Portsmouth has now almost completely vanished. The ruins are only just discernible amongst the trees above the River Taw, near Chulmleigh. Built between 1820 and 1830, abandoned in 1911, the house has stood unwanted and derelict ever since. The processes of decay are almost complete. Within a few more decades the remaining walls will have collapsed, the ivy's stranglehold will be supreme, and Eggesford will be just a memory. Only those who know where to look will be able to find any trace of the house, once one of the most popular meeting places for the nobility and gentry of Devon.

Had it remained the seat of the Portsmouths, would Eggesford perhaps have become the premier showplace of North Devon, a leader in the country-house-open-to-the-public league? Might there have even have been a safari park, a funfair or a collection of ancient motorcars or machinery to attract visitors? As such it would have filled a gap in the attractions of the area, and would have continued to provide a source of employment and wealth to the local population, as it did previously. Speculation, although fascinating, is useless. The Portsmouths preferred their Hampshire possessions, and Eggesford was gone for good.

The Eggesford House, the ruins of which remain, was built by the Hon. Newton Fellowes. The site was magnificent, perched high on the wooded valley slopes with commanding views over the River Taw, North Devon's premier river. Eggesford was in itself a small village, almost self-supporting, complete with courtyards, stableyards, numerous outbuildings and farm buildings. There were two sets of kennels, a school and a school house at Wembworthy, but only one lodge. Down on the main road to Exeter were the Fox and Hounds Hotel, the estate sawmill and the estate laundry. The house itself was large and rambling, built in Victorianized Elizabethan/Gothic style, and differing accounts date it as being built in 1820, 1822, 1828 or 1830. It replaced the former family home down in the valley, close to Eggesford church.

The history of Eggesford is a long one. According to Lyson (1822), the manor's earliest records go back to Henry III, when it belonged to the family of Reigney, from whom it passed to the families of Coplestone and Chichester. The manor house, he tells us, was rebuilt by Edward Lord Chichester in the reign of James I, and the estate passed via the female line to John St. Leger. Risdon's Survey of Devon, dated 1620, is quoted extensively in the parish magazine of 1881.

"In ancient times called Eglesford, of a passage through the river (ford) and goodly woods sometime there, wherein if tradition be taken for truth, eagles bred in our forefathers day. Sir John Reigney held Eggesford in 1233 and eleven Reigneys, called either John or Richard, succeeded in direct line. The last John Reigney had issue, Anne, wife of Charles Coplestone of Bickton, who had issue, John, who died in 1606. This John Coplestone married a daughter of Beeston of Cheshire and had issue, Anne wife of Edward Viscount Chichester of Carrickfergus. This Lord Chichester hath builded a fayre house and dwelleth nowe at Egesford.' Risdon also tells us that Lord Chichester rebuilt the manor-house in the reign of James I (1603-1625). Risdon further tells us that there were two brothers, Sir Arthur and Sir Edward Chichester, the former becoming Baron Chichester of Belfast and the latter Viscount Chichester of Carrickfergus. When Sir Arthur died in 1624 he left his great estates to his brother. Sir Edward's son was created Earl of Donegal and his (Sir Edward's) daughter, Lady Mary, married John St. Leger of Doneraile, County Cork. Their eldest son, Arthur, created Viscount

Doneraile in 1703, was then possessor and inhabitant of Eggesford. The estate was purchased of Arthur St. Leger, Viscount Doneraile in 1718 by William Fellowes, whose grand-daughter, Urania, daughter to Coulson Fellowes, married John, 2nd Earl of Portsmouth whose son was the Hon. Newton Wallop, father of the present Earl of Portsmouth.

It is recorded that Eggesford House was taken by Col. Okey (Cromwell) in the Civil War in 1645. It was rebuilt by William Fellowes who died in 1724 and the Hon. Newton Fellowes had it pulled down and the present Eggesford House built on the site of Heywood, the ancient seat of the Speke family. The present Earl has added a large wing known as the Lymington wing and has affected a great many other improvements."

All traces of the Speke family and their house have long since vanished, but the entry concerning them, again from the 1881 parish book, is worth quoting.

"Wembworthy, a tything adjoining Brushford belonged to the family Le Speke, where they have a house called Heywood, furnished with fair woods, in which the compass of a castle is to be seen between which and the house (as some say) was a passage underground

This family was notable after the conquest as appears from their deeds 'To all their men, French, English or Norman . . ." Sir William Pole remarks that Wembworthy was the ancient dwelling of Speke who have had it from the time of the Conquest. In Henry II's reign, Richard de Espek held five fees. Sir Geoffrey Speke was Lord of Wembworthy in 1620 and about this time he leased Heywood to Sir John Dodderidge, a Justice of the King's Bench. The Manor was sold about 1695 to a Mr. Foote of Tiverton, who left five daughters as co-heiresses. Mr. William Fellowes puchased two shares in 1718, one of which included Heywood. Lord Portsmouth by 1881 had all five shares. The name of Speke still remains at Wembworthy in the crossway, not far from the church, known as Speke's Cross."

The site of the original Eggesford is reputedly the level ground in the grass meadow adjoining the church. According to Polwhele (1797) it was "a brick house built in 1718, and much improved by the present possessor, who also laid out the grounds under the direction of Mr. Richmond." Did William Fellowes himself build a new house in 1718, or did he add to and alter the much older Eggesford, home of the Reigney and Chichester families? If Risdon is believed, Lord Chichester rebuilt his home between 1603 and 1620, but again this could refer to improvements and additions. Whatever the age and fascinating history of the old house, all records appear lost forever, for it was pulled down around 1824 after the new Eggesford was completed. Strangely for so important a property, no-one seems to have any knowledge of its appearance and there are no records of any pictures or prints. The former walled garden remains, and close by Eggesford Barton incorporates the

From the 1913 sale catalogue

stabling and grooms' quarters belonging to the original house. It is possible that the Barton and some of the farm buildings incorporated some of the redundant manor house. A Grade III listed building, Eggesford Barton is described as "mainly 18th century with some re-used materials. Imposing views of battlemented Gothic mansion built about 1830 and dismantled 1917."

Although Eggesford and the Earls of Portsmouth are forever linked in Devonian minds, it should be remembered Eggesford only passed to the Wallop (Portsmouth) family because the third Fellowes, Henry Arthur, died without an heir. It was his sister, Urania, who formed the link between the Wallops and Fellowes and again, had her eldest son, the 3rd Earl, had a son, then the Hampshire and Devonshire estates would not have been merged. Her second son, Newton, changed his name from Wallop to Fellowes in 1794 in order to inherit Eggesford. Perhaps it was the growing certainty that he would eventually also inherit the Portsmouth title and lands that caused him to build his grand new home. Although he is often referred to as the 4th Earl, he held the title for less than one year, dying in January 1854. His wife Catherine, daughter of Earl Fortescue, died the following May and a handsome memorial was erected to them in Eggesford Church. This church, although small, contains a wealth of exceptional family monuments to the various owners and a family vault in which many of the Fellowes and Wallops are buried.

The church itself was restored in 1867 at a cost of £1,000 by the 5th Earl, Isaac Newton Fellowes. He reverted to the family name of Wallop and married Lady Eveline Herbert, daughter of the Earl of Caernarvon. They had twelve children and three of the six sons became in turn the 6th, 7th and 8th Earls. One of their daughters, Lady Rosamund, married Augustus Christie from Tapeley Park at Instow and their son, John Christie the founder of Glyndebourne Opera, was born at Eggesford.

The 5th Earl was a renowned huntsman. In an age that abounded with famous sportsmen, when hunting was the acknowledged sport of the gentry, his passionate enthusiasm for horses, hounds and hunting was outstanding. His father kept a pack of hounds, as did many of the sporting gentry of the day, but on his accession the 5th Earl apparently lost no time in transforming his pack into what was described as 'infinitely superior to anything that has ever been seen in the West of England.' He also kept a pack of otterhounds and both kennels still exist. One of his hunting companions was Parson Jack Russell from Swimbridge and together with various neighbours, including John Moore-Stevens from Winscott, he founded the Chulmleigh Club, meeting at the former Kings Arms where presumably they wiled away the close season by reliving their former exploits in the hunting field.

The lovely story is told of how, following his death in October 1891 at the age of 66 hunting was cancelled for some days as a mark of respect. The first fox to be hunted on resumption found sanctuary in the freshly disturbed earth of the dead earl's grave. As he is buried in the family vault beneath Eggesford church this seems somewhat improbable.

The 6th Earl, Newton, preferred to live at Hurstbourne Park in Hampshire. It was during his time that the break-up of the Devon Estates began and Eggesford was put on the market for the first time. On 14th October, 1913, Knight, Frank and Rutley were

From the 1913 sale catalogue

"directed by the Rt. Hon. Earl of Portsmouth to offer for sale the Freehold, Residential, Sporting and Agricultural Domain of Eggesford estimated to contain 3,277 acres, or thereabouts."

The belief locally is that his father was a gambler and Newton inherited an impoverished estate. The sale catalogue states the Estate was the subject of certain mortgages and other incumbrances and mentions a mortgage of 30th December, 1893 for securing a large sum to the Governors of Queen Anne's Bounty. This bounty had some connection with Tythe redemptions.

Described as a residential property practically unequalled in North Devon, the catalogue preamble continued:

> "a substantially built house of Elizabethan design, a delightful County Seat occupying a beautiful position some 415 ft above sea-level in the centre of a magnificently timbered Park of about 300 acres with panoramic views over the valley of the Taw to the woodland heights beyond. Wide carriage drives, some 2 miles in length, guarded by Lodge Entrances, wind their way through charming woodlands possessing every variety of ornamental shrub and forest tree of exceptional height and dimensions, Avenues of Chestnuts, and

> continuing through the Park terminate at the South-west entrance to the House. The Residence is conveniently planned and contains: Entrance Halls, Long Gallery, Suite of Six Lofty and Spacious Reception Rooms, 30 Bed and Dressing Rooms, exclusive of Men Servants' Rooms, Two Bathrooms, Complete Domestic Offices. Stabling for 40 horses, Cottages, Men's Rooms. Pleasure gardens attractively laid out in Lawns, flower garden and terraces, relieved by clumps of fine rhododendron and azaleas. Walled Kitchen gardens of some 3 acres situated near the site of the old mansion."

Again, the only description left of the interior comes from this catalogue. The entrance hall must have been, to say the least, imposing. A "massive carved door" opened onto the outer hall and granite steps led up to an oak door giving access to a lofty staircase hall with a carved plaster work ceiling, stone fireplace and oak floor. A flight of circular steps terminated at the foot of the wide main staircase with carved newell figures, heads and balusters lighted at the half landing by a tall window. A pair of massive oak glazed doors screened the Long Gallery leading to the principal reception rooms. The gallery was something more than just a corridor, for it measured 64ft. 6ins. in length, by 13ft. 6ins. wide with an oak floor and two stone fireplaces. The drawing room was 30ft. 10ins. by 20ft. 8ins. exclusive of bays and included a deep octagonal-shaped bay. The adjoining stately dining room was of similar size and both rooms were richly panelled, with stone fireplaces. The library was slightly smaller being 20ft. 10ins. square and lined with oak bookcases. Off it was the smoking room. Eggesford incorporated a common feature of Victorian homes, a suite of "men's rooms." A separate corridor led from the main hall to a study, dressing room, bathroom, W.C. and smoking room.

An unusual and much reported feature was the so-called stamp room. This room is mentioned in the particulars but far from being papered throughout with Penny Blacks as has been rumoured, was apparently decorated with patches of various stamps on the walls.

The domestic offices listed a large servants' hall, linen room, dairy, cook's sitting room, spacious kitchen with granite floor, open range, hot plate, charcoal oven, cupboards and shelves, large scullery with stove for scalding cream, copper and sinks, oven pump, plate racks, boiler, larder with meat racks and hooks and spacious cellars under.

On the half landing to the 'Principal Bedchamber Floor' were self-contained suite of boudoir, bedroom, dressing rooms, single bedroom and W.C. On the first floor the State Bedroom measured

From the 1913 sale catalogue

26ft. 9ins. by 15ft. 11ins. excluding bay, with the State Dressing Room, 16ft. 5ins. by 18ft. 10ins., excluding bay. The Oriel room and dressing room were almost as large and there were three other bedrooms.

The North Wing contained five bedrooms, the Nursery Wing two bedrooms, a sitting room and day and night nurseries, and the Servants' Wing had ten bedrooms on two floors.

The main basement was described as well arranged and dry and contained a lamp room, brushing room, W.C. and bathroom, still room, wine cellars, housekeeper's room, butler's pantry with sink, dresser, cupboard and plate cupboard, 2 men's bedroom's, butler's room, boot room. Across the courtyard were a laundry, washing room, store rooms and the Tower room with kitchen and clock tower room.

The main stables, with enclosed yard, contained 8 stalls, corn store, loose box, mess room, harness room with bedroom over, loose box, 5 stalls, 3 boxes, clipping house, harness room with granary over. Round another yard were 6 loose boxes, range of 6 carriage houses, open cart shed with loft, 4 stall stable, corn store with bedroom over, carthorse stable with 6 stalls. The home farmery included a shoeing shed, smith's shop with furnace, bench and anvil, carpenter's shop, mason's shop, cart shed and stable, butchery, 5 loose boxes and stable with 4 stalls.

Water was from a deep well with a large underground cistern for rain water.

One source of water was situated some distance from the house and was pumped up, possibly by donkey or horse power.

The sale included the resident agent's house and Ivy Cottage, the head gardener's cottage, the Fox and Hounds public house, with a rent of £133, six farms of over 200 acres and one of 413 acres, numerous small farms and areas of land, Eggesford saw mills, Eggesford market and the Devon Hunt Kennels. The rent roll was quoted as £3,564 19s. 10d. and the outgoings were the tythe commutation of £208 5s. 5d. and Land Tax of £39 0s. 9d. Sporting rights included six miles of salmon and trout fishing on the River Taw and shooting rights, with the average game bag for the past three seasons quoted:

Average game bag over past 3 seasons.

	1912/13	1911/12	1910/11
Partridges	121	250	100

Pheasants	979	462	755
Wild Duck	48	—	—
Hares	34	32	31
Rabbits	80	76	—
Woodcock	21	20	25
Various	8	2	—

The parkland included 700 acres of woodland, quoted as being some of the finest timber in the county, valued at £40,220 lls. 1d. It does not require too many guesses to name a timber merchant as the purchaser. A newspaper cutting gave the following account of the auction:

> "The estate was sold for £85,000 to Mr. Green of Chesterfield. The rent roll was given as £3,564 19s. 10d. and the timber was valued at £40,220 11s. 1d. The Earl of Portsmouth's asking price was £100,000 but reduced the bidding until an offer of £70,000 was made. The bids rose in £1,000 to £80,000 and then slowly in £500's.
>
> The proceedings took 10 minutes. The purchaser is the senior partner of J.H. & F.W. Green, Timber Merchants, of Whittington, near Chesterfield. The firm have saw mills in Whittington and North Wales and have recently entered into the building trade. This estate was the fifth large estate purchased by Mr. Green within the last 12 months or so."

Within less than a year, on 5th June, 1914, a second auction was held and local memories are often confused between the two. The estate was divided into 83 lots. Eggesford House, Lot 1, was offered for sale but with only 296 acres, and it seems probable that it was on this occasion that the house failed to find a purchaser. In all some 2,763 acres were offered for sale. The Bideford timber firm of Bartlett Bayliss & Co. were reputedly involved in timber-felling operations, but again memories are confused as to whether they were acting for Greens or had bought some of the timber independantly.

The Portsmouth family did not live at Eggesford after about 1911 and no-one now remembers it in its heyday. Some do remember it shut up, empty of furniture, but still kept in good repair. The outbuildings were occupied by German Prisoners of War during 1914/18, and the last person to occupy Eggesford, albeit the servant's wing was a forester. The next owner is named as Squire Luxmore from nearby Dolton who began the gradual process of reducing the mansion to a crumbling ruin. Panelling was removed, fireplaces taken out and and some of the stonework used on his own property. He also removed the clock from the clock tower, donated by local farmers as a mark of gratitude to Lord Portsmouth for

From the 1913 sale catalogue

The Dining Room with portrait of Hon. Newton Fellowes

setting up the local market at Eggesford station. Eggesford is now the property of the Chambers family of Winkleigh.

Eggesford appears not to have suffered the indignity of a demolition sale, but over the years everything that could be utilised was removed and once the roof had been stripped, deterioration was certain. Throughout Devon there are many houses where parts of Eggesford survive and there must be many more where less obvious items than the fireplaces, windows and panelling, were acquired and made use of. Winkleigh village hall was reputedly built from Eggesford's stonework, and the main entrance gates and pillars were re-erected there.

By 1917, only four years after the first sale, a press cutting stated that "the house was stripped of its fittings and the roof removed. The park was cut up and many of the magnificent trees felled."

A sad ending for Eggesford.

The 6th Earl died in 1917 and was succeeded by his brother, John Fellowes Wallop, a bachelor. He had inherited Barton House at

Morchard Bishop from his mother, and continued to live there until his death in September 1925. At one stage he was private secretary to the Governor of Tasmania and is remembered with affection locally. His memorial in Morchard Bishop church reads:

"John Fellowes Wallop, 7th Earl of Portsmouth, Viscount Lymington, Baron Wallop of Farleigh Wallop who — conspicuous for his kindly humour, courtesy, unselfishness, usefulness, energy and courage — devoted the best years of his life to services to the County of Devon." Noblesse oblige indeed. The third brother to inherit, Oliver Henry, had gone out to America in 1884 and was a rancher in Wyoming, married to an American, Marguerite Walker from Kentucky. They returned to England and for a time also lived at Morchard Bishop. But a year after the death of his wife in 1938, the 8th Earl left England and once more crossed the Atlantic. Before he went, the last of the Portsmouth estates in Devon, that once extended to some 20,000 acres, were sold off, including Barton House.

The present Earl (1981) Gerard Vernon Wallop, lived much of his

The ruins c. 1950

life in Kenya. Born in America in May 1898 he has been married twice and has a brother Oliver living in America. The eldest son and heir is Viscount Lymington, Oliver Kintzing Wallop, born in January 1923.

Although most of the magnificent woodlands have gone, much of it during the First World War, the name of Eggesford will be forever associated with trees and timber. It became the first area of land to be afforested in 1919 by the newly formed Forestry Commission, and today Eggesford Forest covers many acres. The planting of the first trees, still growing, is commemorated by a plaque. Fifty years later a second planting took place at which Mrs. Marion Roach participated. She, according to a second plaque, is the daughter of Mr. Tom Brown, M.B.E., the forester mentioned on the first stone and believed to be the last person to live in Eggesford.

Acknowledgements

The author wishes to express her gratitude to the many people who gave her their time and reminiscences; they are too numerous to mention individually but she hopes they will think the result worthwhile.

Thanks are due, also, to the National Trust for permission to reproduce from their booklet on Dunsland House, and to the Country Life magazine for allowing her to quote from Arthur Oswald's article, also on Dunsland House.

Illustrations

Cover photograph of Stevenstone House by Richard Barnett.

Back cover, Yeo Vale House.

A special thank you to all those who allowed the author to borrow their irreplaceable and personal photographs, postcards, etc.

And to the National Monument Record Office in London for many of the illustrations, and Knight, Frank and Rutley of Hanover Square, London for their help with the sale catalogues of Eggesford and Annery.